YOUR ULTIMATE

LOW CARB
HIGH PROTEIN
COOKBOOK

FOR WEIGHT LOSS
AND
MUSCLE BUILDING

ABIGAIL ATKINSON

Table of contents

Welcome and Goals

Welcome to "Your Ultimate Low Carb High Protein Cookbook for Weight Loss and Muscle Building"! This book is designed to help you achieve your goals of weight loss and muscle building while enjoying incredible dishes. You will spend no more than 30 minutes preparing these meals. Let's not waste any time on the path to new goals. So, let's get started:

GOALS

GOAL 1: WEIGHT LOSS AND MUSCLE BUILDING

It is important to maintain a healthy weight and build a strong, muscular body. Our low carb, high protein recipes are specifically designed to help you effectively burn fat and build muscle.

GOAL 2: SIMPLICITY AND SPEED OF PREPARATION

In today's world, time for cooking is often limited. All our recipes can be prepared in 30 minutes or less. This is the perfect solution for busy people who want to eat right without spending hours in the kitchen.

GOAL 3: TASTE AND VARIETY

Healthy eating shouldn't be boring. Every meal should be a pleasure, not a chore. Here you will find various recipes for breakfast, lunch, dinner, snacks, and desserts that will delight not only your body but also your taste buds.

GOAL 4: MINDFULNESS AND JOY IN COOKING

Cooking can be a meditative and relaxing process. We aim to inspire you to enjoy this process, discovering new flavors and experimenting with recipes. Let every step on your path to health be filled with joy and pleasure.

GOAL 5: SUPPORT AND MOTIVATION

We believe that success is easier to achieve when you have support. This book will be your reliable companion and motivator on your journey to reaching your goals. Don't forget to share your successes and reviews—your experience can inspire others.

The Benefits of a Low Carb High Protein Diet

We value your time, which is why this book is designed to help you achieve your weight loss and muscle-building goals while enjoying incredible meals that can be prepared in 30 minutes or less.:

EFFECTIVE WEIGHT LOSS

A low carb high protein diet helps weight loss by reducing insulin levels and promoting fat burning. Lowering carbohydrate intake decreases water retention, leading to a quick drop in weight. Additionally, proteins increase satiety, reducing overall calorie intake.

MUSCLE BUILDING AND MAINTENANCE

Proteins are the building blocks of muscles. A high protein diet supports muscle growth and repair, making it ideal for those engaged in regular physical activity or strength training. This diet helps preserve muscle mass, which is crucial during weight loss.

INCREASED METABOLIC RATE

High protein intake boosts your metabolic rate through a process called thermogenesis. Your body burns more calories to digest and metabolize protein compared to fats and carbohydrates, aiding in weight management and fat loss.

IMPROVED BLOOD SUGAR CONTROL

Reducing carbohydrate intake can lead to improved blood sugar levels and insulin sensitivity. This is particularly beneficial for individuals with type 2 diabetes or those at risk of developing the condition. A stable blood sugar level also means fewer cravings and better energy levels throughout the day.

ENHANCED SATIETY AND APPETITE CONTROL

Proteins are known to reduce appetite and hunger levels, helping you feel fuller for longer periods. This can prevent overeating and unnecessary snacking, support weight loss goals, and promote a healthier eating pattern.

CARDIOVASCULAR HEALTH

A low-carb diet can improve cardiovascular risk factors, including triglycerides, HDL (good) cholesterol, and blood pressure. While it's important to choose healthy protein sources, this dietary approach can contribute to overall cardiovascular health.

SUSTAINABLE ENERGY LEVELS

With fewer carbs, your body shifts to burning fat for energy, leading to more stable and sustainable energy levels. This prevents the energy crashes often associated with high carb diets and helps maintain focus and productivity throughout the day.

REDUCED INFLAMMATION

High protein, low carb diets can reduce inflammation markers in the body. This may lead to decreased risk of chronic diseases and improved overall health and well-being.

Tips for Preparing Meals in 30 Minutes or Less

- **PLAN AHEAD:**

  Invest in kitchen gadgets like a food processor, Instant Pot, or slow cooker. These tools can significantly reduce your cooking time.

- **PREP INGREDIENTS IN ADVANCE:**

  Spend some time on the weekend or during a free evening chopping vegetables, marinating meats, and organizing your ingredients. This way, when it's time to cook, everything is ready to go.

- **USE TIME-SAVING APPLIANCES:**

  Planning your meals for the week can save you a lot of time. Knowing what you'll be cooking daily allows you to prepare ingredients beforehand.

- **KEEP IT SIMPLE:**

  Choose recipes with fewer ingredients and simpler steps. Save complicated recipes for weekends or special occasions.

- **COOK IN BATCHES:**

  Prepare larger quantities of food and store leftovers for future meals. This is especially useful for busy weekdays.

- **USE QUICK-COOKING PROTEINS:**

  Choose proteins that cook quickly, such as chicken breast, fish, shrimp, or ground meats.

- **ONE-PAN MEALS:**

  Opt for one-pan or one-pot meals where everything cooks together. This not only saves time but also reduces cleanup.

- **ORGANIZE YOUR KITCHEN:**

  Keep your kitchen well-organized with frequently used items easily accessible. A well-arranged kitchen can make cooking more efficient.

- **PRACTICE MISE EN PLACE:**

  This French cooking technique involves preparing and organizing all your ingredients before you start cooking. This ensures a smooth and quick cooking process.

Ricotta
and
Smoked Salmon
Stuffed Avocado

 Servings: 2   10 minutes

- *Calories: 310*
- *Protein: 15g*
- *Carbs: 12g*
- *Fat: 24g*

Ingredients:

- 2 ripe avocados, halved and pitted
- 1/2 cup ricotta cheese
- 4 oz smoked salmon, chopped
- 1 tablespoon fresh dill, chopped
- 1 tablespoon lemon juice
- Salt and pepper to taste

Instructions:

1. In a small bowl, mix ricotta cheese, smoked salmon, dill, and lemon juice.
2. Season with salt and pepper to taste.
3. Spoon the mixture into the avocado halves.
4. Serve immediately.

Baked Avocado

with Egg

  Servings: 2   Cook time: 10 minutes

- *Calories: 250*
- *Protein: 10g*
- *Carbohydrates: 8g*
- *Fat: 20g*

Ingredients:

- 1 ripe avocado
- 2 large eggs
- Salt and pepper to taste
- Red pepper flakes (optional)

Instructions:

1. Preheat the oven to 425°F (220°C).
2. Cut the avocado in half and remove the pit.
3. Scoop out a bit of the avocado to make room for the egg.
4. Place the avocado halves in a baking dish and crack an egg into each half.
5. Season with salt, pepper, and red pepper flakes.
6. Bake for 15-20 minutes, until the eggs are set to your liking.

Coconut Matcha Smoothie Bowl

 Servings: 1  5 minutes

- *Calories: 280*
- *Protein: 12g*
- *Carbs: 36g*
- *Fat: 10g*

Ingredients:

- 1/2 cup unsweetened coconut milk
- 1 frozen banana
- 1 tablespoon matcha powder
- 1/4 cup Greek yogurt
- 1 tablespoon chia seeds
- 1 tablespoon unsweetened shredded coconut
- 1 tablespoon pumpkin seeds
- 1/4 cup mixed berries

Instructions:

1. In a blender, combine coconut milk, frozen banana, matcha powder, and Greek yogurt. Blend until smooth.
2. Pour the smoothie into a bowl.
3. Top with chia seeds, shredded coconut, pumpkin seeds, and mixed berries.

Almond Butter and Berry Chia Pudding

 Servings: 2   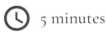 5 minutes

- *Calories (per muffin): 80*
- *Protein: 6g*
- *Carbohydrates: 2g*
- *Fat: 5g*

Ingredients:

- 1/4 cup chia seeds
- 1 cup unsweetened almond milk
- 1 tablespoon almond butter
- 1 tablespoon honey
- 1/2 cup mixed berries

Instructions:

1. In a bowl, combine chia seeds, almond milk, almond butter, and honey. Mix well.
2. Cover and refrigerate overnight.
3. In the morning, stir the pudding and top with mixed berries before serving.

Blueberry Coconut Protein Smoothie

 Servings: 2    5 minutes

- *Calories: 210*
- *Protein: 22g*
- *Carbohydrates: 14g*
- *Fat: 8g*

Ingredients:

- 1 cup fresh or frozen blueberries
- 1/2 cup unsweetened coconut milk
- 1/2 cup plain Greek yogurt
- 1 scoop vanilla protein powder (about 30g)
- 1 tablespoon unsweetened shredded coconut
- 1 tablespoon chia seeds
- 1/2 cup ice cubes
- Sweetener to taste (optional, e.g., stevia or monk fruit sweetener)

Instructions:

1. Add all ingredients (blueberries, coconut milk, Greek yogurt, protein powder, shredded coconut, chia seeds, and ice cubes) into a blender.
2. Blend on high speed until smooth and creamy.
3. Taste and add sweetener if desired, blending again to mix.
4. Pour into two glasses and serve immediately.

Protein Oatmeal Pancake

 Servings: 1   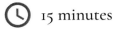 15 minutes

- Calories: 210
- Protein: 20g
- Carbohydrates: 20g
- Fat: 5g

Ingredients:

- 1/2 cup rolled oats
- 1/2 cup cottage cheese
- 3 large egg whites
- 1 teaspoon vanilla extract
- 1/2 teaspoon baking powder
- Cooking spray

Instructions:

1. Blend all ingredients in a blender until smooth.
2. Heat a non-stick skillet over medium heat and lightly grease it with cooking spray.
3. Pour the batter onto the skillet to form a pancake.
4. Cook until bubbles form on the surface, then flip and cook until golden brown on the other side.
5. Serve immediately.

Spicy Turkey
and
Spinach
Breakfast Skillet

 Servings: 2 15 minutes

- *Calories (per muffin): 80*
- *Protein: 6g*
- *Carbohydrates: 2g*
- *Fat: 5g*

Ingredients:

- 1/2 pound ground turkey
- 2 cups fresh spinach
- 1 small red bell pepper, diced
- 1 small onion, diced
- 2 cloves garlic, minced
- 1 tablespoon olive oil
- 1 teaspoon chili flakes
- Salt and pepper to taste

Instructions:

1. Heat olive oil in a skillet over medium heat.
2. Add onion, bell pepper, and garlic. Cook until softened, about 5 minutes.
3. Add ground turkey and cook until browned, about 7 minutes.
4. Stir in spinach and chili flakes, cooking until spinach is wilted.
5. Season with salt and pepper to taste.

Mushroom
and
Spinach
Omelette

  Servings: 1   🕐 15 minutes

- *Calories: 220*
- *Protein: 18g*
- *Carbohydrates: 5g*
- *Fat: 14g*

Ingredients:

- 3 large eggs
- 1/2 cup sliced mushrooms
- 1 cup fresh spinach
- 1/4 cup shredded cheese (optional)
- Salt and pepper to taste
- 1 tablespoon olive oil

Instructions:

1. Heat olive oil in a non-stick skillet over medium heat.
2. Add mushrooms and sauté until they are tender.
3. Add spinach and cook until wilted.
4. In a bowl, whisk the eggs, season with salt and pepper, and pour into the skillet.
5. Cook until the eggs start to set, then sprinkle cheese (if using) on top.
6. Fold the omelette in half and cook until fully set.

Sweet Potato and Chorizo Hash

with Poached Eggs

 Servings: 2 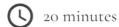 20 minutes

- *Calories: 350*
- *Protein: 18g*
- *Carbs: 25g*
- *Fat: 22g*

Ingredients:

- 1 medium sweet potato, peeled and diced
- 1/2 cup diced chorizo sausage
- 1/2 red bell pepper, diced
- 1/2 green bell pepper, diced
- 1 small red onion, finely chopped
- 2 cloves garlic, minced
- 2 large eggs
- 2 tablespoons olive oil
- 1 tablespoon fresh parsley, chopped
- Salt and pepper to taste

Instructions:

1. Heat olive oil in a large skillet over medium heat.
2. Add sweet potato and cook until it begins to soften, about 5 minutes.
3. Add chorizo, bell peppers, onion, and garlic. Cook for another 10 minutes until the vegetables are tender and the chorizo is browned.
4. In a separate pot, bring water to a simmer. Crack eggs into the water and poach for about 3-4 minutes until whites are set.
5. Serve the hash topped with poached eggs and garnish with fresh parsley, salt, and pepper.

Cottage Cheese Pancakes

with Berries

 Servings: 2   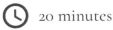 20 minutes

- *Calories: 200*
- *Protein: 16g*
- *Carbohydrates: 15g*
- *Fat: 8g*

Ingredients:

- 1 cup cottage cheese
- 1/2 cup oat flour
- 2 large eggs
- 1/2 teaspoon baking powder
- 1 teaspoon vanilla extract
- 1/2 cup mixed berries

Instructions:

1. In a bowl, mix cottage cheese, oat flour, eggs, baking powder, and vanilla extract until well combined.
2. Heat a non-stick skillet over medium heat and lightly grease it.
3. Pour small amounts of batter onto the skillet to form pancakes.
4. Cook until bubbles form on the surface, then flip and cook until golden brown.
5. Serve with mixed berries on top.

Chia Protein Pudding

 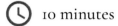 6 Muffins   🕐 10 minutes

- *Calories: 180*
- *Protein: 12g*
- *Carbohydrates: 10g*
- *Fat: 10g*

Ingredients:

- 1 cup unsweetened almond milk
- 1/4 cup chia seeds
- 1 scoop vanilla protein powder
- 1 teaspoon vanilla extract
- 1 tablespoon maple syrup (optional)

Instructions:

1. In a bowl, whisk together almond milk, protein powder, vanilla extract, and maple syrup (if using).
2. Stir in chia seeds.
3. Refrigerate for at least 4 hours or overnight.
4. Stir well before serving.

Chicken
and
Greens
Breakfast Bowl

 Servings: 2   20 minutes

- *Calories: 350*
- *Protein: 30g*
- *Carbohydrates: 12g*
- *Fat: 20g*

Ingredients:

- 1 cup cooked chicken breast, diced
- 2 cups mixed greens (spinach, kale, arugula)
- 1/2 avocado, sliced
- 1/4 cup cherry tomatoes, halved
- 2 tablespoons olive oil
- 1 tablespoon balsamic vinegar
- Salt and pepper to taste

Instructions:

1. In a large bowl, combine mixed greens, chicken, avocado, and cherry tomatoes.
2. Drizzle with olive oil and balsamic vinegar.
3. Toss gently to combine and season with salt and pepper.

Poached Eggs

with Smoked Salmon

 Servings: 1   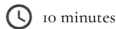 10 minutes

- *Calories: 250*
- *Protein: 18g*
- *Carbohydrates: 6g*
- *Fat: 18g*

Ingredients:

- 2 large eggs
- 2 slices smoked salmon
- 1/2 avocado, sliced
- 1 tablespoon chopped fresh dill
- Salt and pepper to taste

Instructions:

1. Fill a saucepan with water and bring to a gentle simmer.
2. Crack the eggs into individual bowls.
3. Create a gentle whirlpool in the water and gently slide the eggs into the center.
4. Poach for about 3-4 minutes, until the whites are set.
5. Remove the eggs with a slotted spoon and place on a plate with smoked salmon and avocado.
6. Sprinkle with fresh dill and season with salt and pepper.

Keto Waffles

 4 waffles 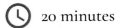 20 minutes

- Calories: 250
- Protein: 12g
- Carbohydrates: 8g
- Fat: 20g

Ingredients:

- 1 cup almond flour
- 1/4 cup coconut flour
- 1 teaspoon baking powder
- 3 large eggs
- 1/4 cup unsweetened almond milk
- 1/4 cup melted coconut oil
- 1 teaspoon vanilla extract

Instructions:

1. Preheat your waffle iron.
2. In a bowl, mix almond flour, coconut flour, and baking powder.
3. In another bowl, whisk together the eggs, almond milk, coconut oil, and vanilla extract.
4. Combine wet and dry ingredients and mix well.
5. Pour batter into the preheated waffle iron and cook according to the manufacturer's instructions until golden brown.
6. Serve immediately.

Mini Bacon Omelettes

 6 omelettes  25 minutes

- *Calories: 150*
- *Protein: 10g*
- *Carbohydrates: 1g*
- *Fat: 12g*

Ingredients:

- 6 large eggs
- 1/2 cup diced cooked bacon
- 1/2 cup shredded cheddar cheese
- 1/4 cup chopped green onions
- Salt and pepper to taste
- Cooking spray

Instructions:

1. Preheat the oven to 375°F (190°C). Spray a muffin tin with cooking spray.
2. In a bowl, whisk the eggs and season with salt and pepper.
3. Stir in the diced bacon, shredded cheese, and chopped green onions.
4. Pour the mixture evenly into the muffin tin cups.
5. Bake for 15 minutes, or until the omelettes are set and lightly browned on top.
6. Let cool slightly before removing from the tin.

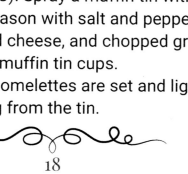

Protein Balls
with Nuts

 12 balls 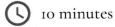 10 minutes

- Calories: 100
- Protein: 5g
- Carbohydrates: 10g
- Fat: 5g

Ingredients:

- 1 cup rolled oats
- 1/2 cup peanut butter or almond butter
- 1/4 cup honey or maple syrup
- 1/2 cup protein powder
- 1/4 cup chopped nuts (almonds, walnuts, etc.)
- 1/4 cup dark chocolate chips (optional)

Instructions:

1. In a large bowl, mix all the ingredients until well combined.
2. Roll the mixture into 12 balls.
3. Place the balls on a baking sheet lined with parchment paper and refrigerate for at least 30 minutes before serving.

Hummus

with Carrot Sticks

 Servings: 4    10 minutes

- *Calories: 200*
- *Protein: 6g*
- *Carbohydrates: 20g*
- *Fat: 10g*

Ingredients:

- 1 can (15 oz) chickpeas, drained and rinsed
- 1/4 cup tahini
- 2 tablespoons olive oil
- 2 cloves garlic, minced
- Juice of 1 lemon
- Salt and pepper to taste
- 4 large carrots, cut into sticks

Instructions:

1. In a food processor, combine chickpeas, tahini, olive oil, garlic, lemon juice, salt, and pepper.
2. Blend until smooth, adding water as needed to reach the desired consistency.
3. Serve the hummus with carrot sticks.

Greek Yogurt
with Nuts and Berries

 Servings: 1  5 minutes

- *Calories: 220*
- *Protein: 18g*
- *Carbohydrates: 15g*
- *Fat: 10g*

Ingredients:

- 1 cup Greek yogurt
- 1/4 cup mixed berries (strawberries, blueberries, raspberries)
- 2 tablespoons chopped nuts (almonds, walnuts, etc.)
- 1 tablespoon honey (optional)

Instructions:

1. In a bowl, combine Greek yogurt, mixed berries, and chopped nuts.
2. Drizzle with honey if desired.
3. Serve immediately.

Avocado Rolls
with Tuna

 4 rolls   🕐 10 minutes

- *Calories: 150*
- *Protein: 12g*
- *Carbohydrates: 6g*
- *Fat: 10g*

Ingredients:

- 1 avocado, sliced
- 1 can (5 oz) tuna, drained
- 1 tablespoon mayonnaise
- 1 teaspoon Dijon mustard
- 1 cucumber, sliced into thin strips
- Salt and pepper to taste
- Seaweed sheets (nori) or lettuce leaves for wrapping

Instructions:

1. In a bowl, mix the tuna, mayonnaise, Dijon mustard, salt, and pepper.
2. Lay out a seaweed sheet or lettuce leaf and place avocado slices and cucumber strips on it.
3. Add a spoonful of the tuna mixture on top.
4. Roll tightly and slice into bite-sized pieces.

Protein Bars

 8 bars 🕐 10 minutes

- Calories: 200
- Protein: 10g
- Carbohydrates: 18g
- Fat: 10g

Ingredients:

- 1 cup rolled oats
- 1/2 cup almond butter
- 1/4 cup honey or maple syrup
- 1/2 cup protein powder
- 1/4 cup dark chocolate chips (optional)

Instructions:

1. In a large bowl, mix all the ingredients until well combined.
2. Press the mixture into an 8x8 inch baking dish lined with parchment paper.
3. Refrigerate for at least 1 hour before cutting into bars.

Cheese Chips

 Servings: 4   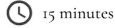 15 minutes

- *Calories: 120*
- *Protein: 7g*
- *Carbohydrates: 1g*
- *Fat: 10g*

Ingredients:

- 1 cup shredded cheddar cheese
- 1/2 teaspoon garlic powder
- 1/2 teaspoon paprika

Instructions:

1. Preheat the oven to 400°F (200°C). Line a baking sheet with parchment paper.
2. Place small mounds of shredded cheese on the baking sheet, leaving space between each mound.
3. Sprinkle with garlic powder and paprika.
4. Bake for 5-10 minutes, or until the cheese is melted and crispy.
5. Let cool before serving.

Veggie Rolls
with Chicken

 4 rolls   🕐 15 minutes

- *Calories: 120*
- *Protein: 14g*
- *Carbohydrates: 6g*
- *Fat: 6g*

Ingredients:

- 1 cup cooked chicken breast, shredded
- 1 carrot, julienned
- 1 cucumber, julienned
- 1 avocado, sliced
- Lettuce leaves for wrapping
- 1 tablespoon soy sauce
- 1 teaspoon sesame oil

Instructions:

1. In a bowl, mix the shredded chicken with soy sauce and sesame oil.
2. Lay out a lettuce leaf and place carrot, cucumber, and avocado on it.
3. Add a spoonful of the chicken mixture on top.
4. Roll tightly and slice into bite-sized pieces.

Nut Mix

 Servings: 4    5 minutes

- *Calories: 200*
- *Protein: 6g*
- *Carbohydrates: 12g*
- *Fat: 16g*

Ingredients:

- 1/2 cup almonds
- 1/2 cup walnuts
- 1/2 cup cashews
- 1/4 cup pumpkin seeds
- 1/4 cup dried cranberries (optional)

Instructions:

1. In a bowl, mix all the ingredients together.
2. Store in an airtight container.

Protein Shake

 Servings: 1   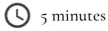 5 minutes

- *Calories: 250*
- *Protein: 20g*
- *Carbohydrates: 15g*
- *Fat: 12g*

Ingredients:

- 1 cup unsweetened almond milk
- 1 scoop chocolate protein powder
- 1 tablespoon peanut butter
- 1/2 banana
- Ice cubes (optional)

Instructions:

1. Combine all ingredients in a blender.
2. Blend until smooth.
3. Serve immediately.

Chicken Breasts
with Broccoli

 Servings: 4    30 minutes

- *Calories: 290*
- *Protein: 35g*
- *Carbohydrates: 6g*
- *Fat: 14g*

Ingredients:

- 4 boneless, skinless chicken breasts
- 2 cups broccoli florets
- 2 tablespoons olive oil
- 2 cloves garlic, minced
- Salt and pepper to taste
- 1 teaspoon paprika

Instructions:

1. Preheat the oven to 375°F (190°C).
2. Place the chicken breasts on a baking sheet and drizzle with olive oil.
3. Sprinkle with garlic, salt, pepper, and paprika.
4. Add the broccoli florets around the chicken.
5. Bake for 20 minutes, or until the chicken is cooked through and the broccoli is tender.

Grilled Salmon

with Asparagus

 Servings: 4 30 minutes

- Calories: 350
- Protein: 30g
- Carbohydrates: 6g
- Fat: 22g

Ingredients:

- 4 salmon fillets
- 1 bunch asparagus, trimmed
- 2 tablespoons olive oil
- 1 lemon, sliced
- Salt and pepper to taste
- 1 teaspoon dried dill

Instructions:

1. Preheat the grill to medium-high heat.
2. Brush the salmon fillets and asparagus with olive oil and season with salt, pepper, and dill.
3. Grill the salmon for 4-5 minutes on each side, or until cooked to your liking.
4. Grill the asparagus for 5-7 minutes, turning occasionally, until tender.
5. Serve with lemon slices.

Chicken Salad
with Avocado

  Servings: 4   🕐 15 minutes

- Calories: 320
- Protein: 28g
- Carbohydrates: 10g
- Fat: 20g

Ingredients:

- 2 cups cooked chicken breast, shredded
- 2 avocados, diced
- 1 cup cherry tomatoes, halved
- 1/4 cup red onion, finely chopped
- 2 tablespoons lime juice
- 2 tablespoons olive oil
- Salt and pepper to taste
- Fresh cilantro for garnish

Instructions:

1. In a large bowl, combine the chicken, avocados, cherry tomatoes, and red onion.
2. In a small bowl, whisk together the lime juice, olive oil, salt, and pepper.
3. Pour the dressing over the salad and toss gently to combine.
4. Garnish with fresh cilantro and serve.

Tuna
with Green Salad

 Servings: 2   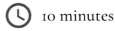 10 minutes

- *Calories: 250*
- *Protein: 28g*
- *Carbohydrates: 8g*
- *Fat: 12g*

Ingredients:

- 2 cans (5 oz each) tuna, drained
- 4 cups mixed greens
- 1/2 cucumber, sliced
- 1/2 red bell pepper, sliced
- 1/4 cup red onion, sliced
- 1 avocado, sliced
- 2 tablespoons olive oil
- 1 tablespoon lemon juice
- Salt and pepper to taste

Instructions:

1. In a large bowl, combine the mixed greens, cucumber, bell pepper, red onion, and avocado.
2. Top with the drained tuna.
3. In a small bowl, whisk together the olive oil, lemon juice, salt, and pepper.
4. Drizzle the dressing over the salad and toss gently to combine.

Beef Steak

with Vegetables

 Servings: 2   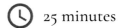 25 minutes

- Calories: 400
- Protein: 40g
- Carbohydrates: 8g
- Fat: 22g

Ingredients:

- 2 beef steaks (6 oz each)
- 1 cup broccoli florets
- 1 cup bell pepper slices
- 1 cup zucchini slices
- 2 tablespoons olive oil
- Salt and pepper to taste
- 1 teaspoon garlic powder

Instructions:

1. Preheat a grill or skillet to medium-high heat.
2. Brush the steaks with 1 tablespoon olive oil and season with salt, pepper, and garlic powder.
3. Grill the steaks for 5-7 minutes on each side, or until cooked to your liking.
4. Meanwhile, in a separate skillet, heat the remaining olive oil over medium heat.
5. Add the broccoli, bell pepper, and zucchini, and sauté until tender.
6. Serve the steaks with the sautéed vegetables.

Chicken
with Cauliflower

 Servings: 4   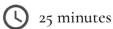 25 minutes

- *Calories: 320*
- *Protein: 28g*
- *Carbohydrates: 6g*
- *Fat: 20g*

Ingredients:

- 4 boneless, skinless chicken thighs
- 2 cups cauliflower florets
- 2 tablespoons olive oil
- 2 cloves garlic, minced
- 1 teaspoon paprika
- Salt and pepper to taste
- Fresh parsley for garnish

Instructions:

1. Heat olive oil in a large skillet over medium-high heat.
2. Season the chicken thighs with salt, pepper, and paprika.
3. Add the chicken to the skillet and cook for 5-7 minutes on each side, or until fully cooked.
4. Add the cauliflower florets and garlic to the skillet and sauté for an additional 5 minutes, or until tender.
5. Garnish with fresh parsley and serve.

Pork

with

Brussels Sprouts

 Servings: 4   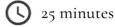 25 minutes

- Calories: 350
- Protein: 30g
- Carbohydrates: 8g
- Fat: 22g

Ingredients:

- 4 boneless pork chops
- 2 cups Brussels sprouts, halved
- 2 tablespoons olive oil
- 2 cloves garlic, minced
- Salt and pepper to taste
- 1 teaspoon thyme

Instructions:

1. Heat olive oil in a large skillet over medium-high heat.
2. Season the pork chops with salt, pepper, and thyme.
3. Add the pork chops to the skillet and cook for 5-7 minutes on each side, or until fully cooked.
4. Add the Brussels sprouts and garlic to the skillet and sauté for an additional 5 minutes, or until tender.
5. Serve immediately.

Turkey
Salad
with Nuts

 Servings: 4   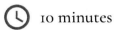 10 minutes

- *Calories: 300*
- *Protein: 28g*
- *Carbohydrates: 10g*
- *Fat: 18g*

Ingredients:

- 2 cups cooked turkey breast, diced
- 4 cups mixed greens
- 1/4 cup chopped nuts (almonds, walnuts, etc.)
- 1/4 cup dried cranberries (optional)
- 1/4 cup crumbled feta cheese (optional)
- 2 tablespoons olive oil
- 1 tablespoon balsamic vinegar
- Salt and pepper to taste

Instructions:

1. In a large bowl, combine the turkey, mixed greens, nuts, cranberries, and feta cheese.
2. In a small bowl, whisk together the olive oil, balsamic vinegar, salt, and pepper.
3. Pour the dressing over the salad and toss gently to combine.
4. Serve immediately.

Vegetable Stew
with Chicken

 Servings: 4   🕐 30 minutes

- *Calories: 250*
- *Protein: 28g*
- *Carbohydrates: 12g*
- *Fat: 10g*

Ingredients:

- 2 cups cooked chicken breast, diced
- 1 cup diced carrots
- 1 cup diced celery
- 1 cup diced tomatoes
- 1 cup chopped kale
- 4 cups chicken broth
- 2 cloves garlic, minced
- 1 tablespoon olive oil
- Salt and pepper to taste
- 1 teaspoon thyme

Instructions:

1. Heat olive oil in a large pot over medium heat.
2. Add the carrots, celery, and garlic, and sauté for 5 minutes.
3. Add the diced tomatoes, chicken broth, and thyme, and bring to a boil.
4. Reduce the heat and simmer for 10 minutes.
5. Add the cooked chicken and kale, and cook for an additional 5 minutes.
6. Season with salt and pepper to taste, and serve.

Turkey Meatballs

with Tomato Sauce

 Servings: 4   🕐 30 minutes

- Calories: 320
- Protein: 28g
- Carbohydrates: 10g
- Fat: 18g

Ingredients:

- 1 pound ground turkey
- 1/4 cup grated Parmesan cheese
- 1/4 cup almond flour
- 1 egg
- 2 cloves garlic, minced
- 1 teaspoon Italian seasoning
- Salt and pepper to taste
- 2 cups marinara sauce

Instructions:

1. In a bowl, combine the ground turkey, Parmesan cheese, almond flour, egg, garlic, Italian seasoning, salt, and pepper.
2. Form the mixture into meatballs.
3. Heat a large skillet over medium-high heat and add the meatballs.
4. Cook until browned on all sides, about 10 minutes.
5. Add the marinara sauce to the skillet and simmer for 10 minutes.
6. Serve with your favorite low-carb side.

Keto Noodles
with Shrimp

 Servings: 4   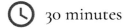 30 minutes

- Calories: 250
- Protein: 28g
- Carbohydrates: 6g
- Fat: 12g

Ingredients:

- 1 pound shrimp, peeled and deveined
- 2 zucchinis, spiralized into noodles
- 2 tablespoons olive oil
- 2 cloves garlic, minced
- 1/4 cup grated Parmesan cheese
- 1/4 cup chopped parsley
- Salt and pepper to taste

Instructions:

1. Heat olive oil in a large skillet over medium heat.
2. Add the garlic and shrimp, and cook until the shrimp are pink and opaque, about 5 minutes.
3. Add the zucchini noodles and cook for an additional 3-4 minutes, until tender.
4. Remove from heat and stir in Parmesan cheese and parsley.
5. Season with salt and pepper to taste, and serve.

Pollock Fillets
with Herbs

 Servings: 4   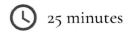 25 minutes

- Calories: 220
- Protein: 28g
- Carbohydrates: 2g
- Fat: 10g

Ingredients:

- 4 pollock fillets
- 2 tablespoons olive oil
- 2 cloves garlic, minced
- 1 lemon, sliced
- 1 teaspoon dried dill
- Salt and pepper to taste

Instructions:

1. Preheat the oven to 375°F (190°C).
2. Place the pollock fillets on a baking sheet and drizzle with olive oil.
3. Sprinkle with garlic, dill, salt, and pepper.
4. Arrange lemon slices on top of the fillets.
5. Bake for 15 minutes, or until the fish is cooked through and flakes easily with a fork.
6. Serve immediately.

Tofu Scramble
with Vegetables

 Servings: 4   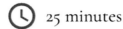 25 minutes

- *Calories: 180*
- *Protein: 14g*
- *Carbohydrates: 8g*
- *Fat: 12g*

Ingredients:

- 1 block firm tofu, drained and crumbled
- 1 cup diced bell peppers
- 1 cup spinach leaves
- 1/2 cup diced tomatoes
- 1/4 cup chopped onion
- 2 tablespoons olive oil
- 1 teaspoon turmeric
- Salt and pepper to taste

Instructions:

1. Heat olive oil in a large skillet over medium heat.
2. Add the onion and bell peppers, and sauté until tender, about 5 minutes.
3. Add the crumbled tofu and turmeric, and cook for an additional 5 minutes.
4. Stir in the spinach and tomatoes, and cook until the spinach is wilted.
5. Season with salt and pepper to taste, and serve.

Tilapia
with Lemon and Garlic

 Servings: 4   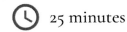 25 minutes

- *Calories: 210*
- *Protein: 28g*
- *Carbohydrates: 2g*
- *Fat: 10g*

Ingredients:

- 4 tilapia fillets
- 2 tablespoons olive oil
- 2 cloves garlic, minced
- 1 lemon, sliced
- Salt and pepper to taste
- Fresh parsley for garnish

Instructions:

1. Preheat the oven to 375°F (190°C).
2. Place the tilapia fillets on a baking sheet and drizzle with olive oil.
3. Sprinkle with garlic, salt, and pepper.
4. Arrange lemon slices on top of the fillets.
5. Bake for 15 minutes, or until the fish is cooked through and flakes easily with a fork.
6. Garnish with fresh parsley and serve.

Garlic Baked Chicken

Servings: 4   25 minutes

- Calories: 250
- Protein: 30g
- Carbohydrates: 2g
- Fat: 12g

Ingredients:

- 4 boneless, skinless chicken breasts
- 4 cloves garlic, minced
- 2 tablespoons olive oil
- 1 teaspoon dried oregano
- Salt and pepper to taste
- Fresh parsley for garnish

Instructions:

1. Preheat the oven to 400°F (200°C).
2. In a small bowl, mix the garlic, olive oil, oregano, salt, and pepper.
3. Place the chicken breasts in a baking dish and spread the garlic mixture over them.
4. Bake for 20 minutes, or until the chicken is cooked through.
5. Garnish with fresh parsley and serve.

Beef
with Green Beans

 Servings: 4   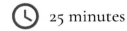 25 minutes

- Calories: 300
- Protein: 28g
- Carbohydrates: 6g
- Fat: 18g

Ingredients:

- 1 lb (450g) beef sirloin, thinly sliced
- 2 cups green beans, trimmed
- 2 tablespoons olive oil
- 2 cloves garlic, minced
- 1 tablespoon soy sauce
- Salt and pepper to taste

Instructions:

1. Heat olive oil in a large skillet over medium-high heat.
2. Add the garlic and beef slices, and cook until the beef is browned.
3. Add the green beans and soy sauce, and cook for an additional 5 minutes, until the beans are tender.
4. Season with salt and pepper to taste and serve.

Citrus Crusted Salmon

 Servings: 4 25 minutes

- Calories: 320
- Protein: 28g
- Carbohydrates: 4g
- Fat: 20g

Ingredients:

- 4 salmon fillets
- 1 orange, zested and juiced
- 1 lemon, zested and juiced
- 2 tablespoons olive oil
- Salt and pepper to taste
- Fresh dill for garnish

Instructions:

1. Preheat the oven to 400°F (200°C).
2. In a small bowl, mix the orange zest and juice, lemon zest and juice, olive oil, salt, and pepper.
3. Place the salmon fillets on a baking sheet and brush with the citrus mixture.
4. Bake for 15 minutes, or until the salmon is cooked through.
5. Garnish with fresh dill and serve.

Teriyaki Chicken Thighs

 Servings: 4   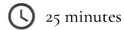 25 minutes

- *Calories: 290*
- *Protein: 26g*
- *Carbohydrates: 6g*
- *Fat: 18g*

Ingredients:

- 8 boneless, skinless chicken thighs
- 1/4 cup soy sauce
- 2 tablespoons honey or a low-carb sweetener
- 2 cloves garlic, minced
- 1 teaspoon grated ginger
- 1 tablespoon sesame oil
- 1 tablespoon sesame seeds (optional)
- Chopped green onions for garnish

Instructions:

1. In a small bowl, mix the soy sauce, honey, garlic, ginger, and sesame oil.
2. Heat a large skillet over medium-high heat and add the chicken thighs.
3. Cook the chicken for 5 minutes on each side, until browned.
4. Pour the teriyaki sauce over the chicken and cook for an additional 5 minutes, until the chicken is fully cooked and the sauce is thickened.
5. Sprinkle with sesame seeds and chopped green onions before serving.

Keto Meat Lasagna

 Servings: 6   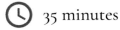 35 minutes

- *Calories: 350*
- *Protein: 28g*
- *Carbohydrates: 8g*
- *Fat: 22g*

Ingredients:

- 1 lb (450g) ground beef
- 1 cup marinara sauce (no sugar added)
- 2 cups ricotta cheese
- 2 cups shredded mozzarella cheese
- 1 egg
- 2 zucchinis, thinly sliced lengthwise
- 1 teaspoon Italian seasoning
- Salt and pepper to taste

Instructions:

1. Preheat the oven to 375°F (190°C).
2. In a skillet, cook the ground beef over medium heat until browned. Drain any excess fat.
3. Add the marinara sauce to the beef and simmer for 5 minutes.
4. In a bowl, mix the ricotta cheese, egg, Italian seasoning, salt, and pepper.
5. In a baking dish, layer the zucchini slices, ricotta mixture, beef mixture, and mozzarella cheese.
6. Repeat the layers, ending with a layer of mozzarella cheese.
7. Bake for 20 minutes, or until the cheese is melted and bubbly.

Garlic Lemon Shrimp

 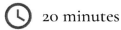 Servings: 4   🕐 20 minutes

- Calories: 200
- Protein: 24g
- Carbohydrates: 2g
- Fat: 10g

Ingredients:

- 1 lb (450g) shrimp, peeled and deveined
- 2 tablespoons olive oil
- 3 cloves garlic, minced
- Juice of 1 lemon
- 1 tablespoon chopped parsley
- Salt and pepper to taste

Instructions:

1. Heat olive oil in a large skillet over medium-high heat.
2. Add the garlic and cook for 1 minute, until fragrant.
3. Add the shrimp and cook for 2-3 minutes on each side, until pink and opaque.
4. Squeeze lemon juice over the shrimp and sprinkle with parsley.
5. Season with salt and pepper to taste and serve.

Pork

with Mushroom Sauce

 Servings: 4   25 minutes

- *Calories: 350*
- *Protein: 30g*
- *Carbohydrates: 4g*
- *Fat: 22g*

Ingredients:

- 4 boneless pork chops
- 2 tablespoons olive oil
- 1 cup sliced mushrooms
- 1/2 cup chicken broth
- 1/4 cup heavy cream
- 1 teaspoon Dijon mustard
- Salt and pepper to taste
- Fresh thyme for garnish

Instructions:

1. Heat olive oil in a large skillet over medium-high heat.
2. Season the pork chops with salt and pepper and add to the skillet.
3. Cook for 5-7 minutes on each side, until fully cooked.
4. Remove the pork chops and set aside.
5. Add the mushrooms to the skillet and cook for 5 minutes, until tender.
6. Stir in the chicken broth, heavy cream, and Dijon mustard.
7. Simmer for 3-5 minutes, until the sauce thickens.
8. Return the pork chops to the skillet and coat with the sauce.
9. Garnish with fresh thyme and serve.

Grilled Tuna
with Lemon Sauce

 Servings: 4   🕐 25 minutes

- Calories: 280
- Protein: 32g
- Carbohydrates: 2g
- Fat: 16g

Ingredients:

- 4 tuna steaks
- 2 tablespoons olive oil
- Juice of 1 lemon
- 1 tablespoon soy sauce
- 1 teaspoon grated ginger
- Salt and pepper to taste

Instructions:

1. Preheat the grill to medium-high heat.
2. In a small bowl, mix the olive oil, lemon juice, soy sauce, ginger, salt, and pepper.
3. Brush the tuna steaks with the lemon sauce mixture.
4. Grill the tuna for 3-4 minutes on each side, or until cooked to your liking.
5. Serve with additional lemon sauce if desired.

Chicken
with Tomatoes and Basil

 Servings: 4 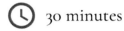 30 minutes

- *Calories: 280*
- *Protein: 30g*
- *Carbohydrates: 6g*
- *Fat: 14g*

Ingredients:

- 4 boneless, skinless chicken breasts
- 2 cups cherry tomatoes, halved
- 2 cloves garlic, minced
- 2 tablespoons olive oil
- 1/4 cup fresh basil leaves, chopped
- Salt and pepper to taste
- 1/4 cup grated Parmesan cheese (optional)

Instructions:

1. Preheat the oven to 400°F (200°C).
2. In a baking dish, place the chicken breasts and drizzle with olive oil.
3. Add the cherry tomatoes and garlic around the chicken.
4. Season with salt and pepper.
5. Bake for 20 minutes, or until the chicken is cooked through.
6. Sprinkle with fresh basil and Parmesan cheese (if using) before serving.

Beef Meatballs in Sauce

 Servings: 4    25 minutes

- Calories: 320
- Protein: 28g
- Carbohydrates: 10g
- Fat: 18g

Ingredients:

- 1 lb (450g) ground beef
- 1/4 cup grated Parmesan cheese
- 1/4 cup almond flour
- 1 egg
- 2 cloves garlic, minced
- 1 teaspoon Italian seasoning
- Salt and pepper to taste
- 2 cups marinara sauce (no sugar added)

Instructions:

1. In a bowl, combine the ground beef, Parmesan cheese, almond flour, egg, garlic, Italian seasoning, salt, and pepper.
2. Form the mixture into meatballs.
3. Heat a large skillet over medium-high heat and add the meatballs.
4. Cook until browned on all sides, about 10 minutes.
5. Add the marinara sauce to the skillet and simmer for 10 minutes.
6. Serve with your favorite low-carb side.

Chicken Vegetable Soup

 Servings: 4 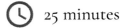 25 minutes

- *Calories: 230*
- *Protein: 28g*
- *Carbohydrates: 8g*
- *Fat: 10g*

Ingredients:

- 2 cups cooked chicken breast, shredded
- 4 cups chicken broth
- 1 cup diced carrots
- 1 cup diced celery
- 1 cup spinach leaves
- 2 cloves garlic, minced
- 1 tablespoon olive oil
- Salt and pepper to taste
- 1 teaspoon oregano

Instructions:

1. Heat olive oil in a large pot over medium heat.
2. Add the carrots, celery, and garlic, and sauté for 5 minutes.
3. Add the chicken broth and oregano, and bring to a boil.
4. Reduce the heat and simmer for 10 minutes.
5. Add the shredded chicken and spinach, and cook for an additional 5 minutes.
6. Season with salt and pepper to taste, and serve.

Halibut Fillets
with Herbs

 Servings: 4   🕐 25 minutes

- Calories: 220
- Protein: 28g
- Carbohydrates: 2g
- Fat: 10g

Ingredients:

- 4 halibut fillets
- 2 tablespoons olive oil
- 2 cloves garlic, minced
- 1 lemon, sliced
- 1 teaspoon dried dill
- Salt and pepper to taste

Instructions:

1. Preheat the oven to 375°F (190°C).
2. Place the halibut fillets on a baking sheet and drizzle with olive oil.
3. Sprinkle with garlic, dill, salt, and pepper.
4. Arrange lemon slices on top of the fillets.
5. Bake for 15 minutes, or until the fish is cooked through and flakes easily with a fork.
6. Serve immediately.

Chicken Skewers

with Vegetables

 Servings: 4　　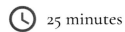 25 minutes

- *Calories: 250*
- *Protein: 28g*
- *Carbohydrates: 6g*
- *Fat: 12g*

Ingredients:

- 1 lb (450g) chicken breast, cut into cubes
- 1 red bell pepper, cut into squares
- 1 green bell pepper, cut into squares
- 1 red onion, cut into squares
- 2 tablespoons olive oil
- 2 cloves garlic, minced
- Salt and pepper to taste
- 1 teaspoon paprika

Instructions:

1. Preheat the grill to medium-high heat.
2. In a bowl, mix the olive oil, garlic, salt, pepper, and paprika.
3. Thread the chicken and vegetables onto skewers.
4. Brush with the olive oil mixture.
5. Grill for 10-15 minutes, turning occasionally, until the chicken is cooked through.
6. Serve immediately.

Keto Pizza

 Servings: 4   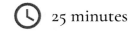 25 minutes

- *Calories: 350*
- *Protein: 20g*
- *Carbohydrates: 8g*
- *Fat: 28g*

Ingredients:

- 1 cup almond flour
- 1/4 cup coconut flour
- 1 teaspoon baking powder
- 2 large eggs
- 1/4 cup unsweetened almond milk
- 1/4 cup shredded mozzarella cheese
- 1/4 cup marinara sauce (no sugar added)
- 1/2 cup sliced pepperoni
- 1/2 cup sliced bell peppers
- 1/2 cup sliced mushrooms
- 1/4 cup grated Parmesan cheese
- 1 teaspoon Italian seasoning

Instructions:

1. Preheat the oven to 375°F (190°C).
2. In a bowl, mix the almond flour, coconut flour, baking powder, eggs, and almond milk to form a dough.
3. Press the dough onto a baking sheet lined with parchment paper to form a pizza crust.
4. Bake for 10 minutes, until lightly browned.
5. Spread the marinara sauce over the crust and top with mozzarella cheese, pepperoni, bell peppers, mushrooms, Parmesan cheese, and Italian seasoning.
6. Bake for an additional 10 minutes, or until the cheese is melted and bubbly.
7. Serve immediately.

Tuna Salad
with Olives

 Servings: 4   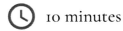 10 minutes

- Calories: 220
- Protein: 20g
- Carbohydrates: 2g
- Fat: 14g

Ingredients:

- 2 cans (5 oz each) tuna, drained
- 1/4 cup mayonnaise
- 1 tablespoon lemon juice
- 1/4 cup chopped green olives
- 1/4 cup chopped red onion
- Salt and pepper to taste
- Fresh parsley for garnish

Instructions:

1. In a bowl, combine the tuna, mayonnaise, lemon juice, green olives, red onion, salt, and pepper.
2. Mix well until all ingredients are combined.
3. Garnish with fresh parsley and serve.

Protein Chocolate Mousse

 Servings: 4 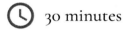 30 minutes

- *Calories: 120*
- *Protein: 15g*
- *Carbohydrates: 8g*
- *Fat: 4g*

Ingredients:

- 1 cup Greek yogurt
- 2 tablespoons cocoa powder
- 2 tablespoons protein powder (chocolate flavor)
- 1 tablespoon honey or a low-carb sweetener
- 1 teaspoon vanilla extract
- Dark chocolate shavings for garnish (optional)

Instructions:

1. In a bowl, mix together Greek yogurt, cocoa powder, protein powder, honey, and vanilla extract until smooth.
2. Divide the mixture into serving cups.
3. Refrigerate for at least 20 minutes to set.
4. Garnish with dark chocolate shavings before serving, if desired.

Low Carb Cheesecake

 Servings: 8   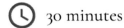 30 minutes

- *Calories: 220*
- *Protein: 8g*
- *Carbohydrates: 4g*
- *Fat: 18g*

Ingredients:

- 2 cups cream cheese, softened
- 1/2 cup sour cream
- 2 eggs
- 1/2 cup granulated sweetener (such as erythritol)
- 1 teaspoon vanilla extract
- Zest of 1 lemon
- Fresh berries for garnish

Instructions:

1. Preheat the oven to 325°F (160°C).
2. In a bowl, beat together cream cheese, sour cream, eggs, sweetener, vanilla extract, and lemon zest until smooth.
3. Pour the mixture into a greased pie dish.
4. Bake for 20 minutes, or until the edges are set but the center is slightly jiggly.
5. Allow to cool completely, then refrigerate for at least 2 hours before serving.
6. Garnish with fresh berries before serving.

Keto
Brownies

 Servings: 9    30 minutes

- Calories: 220
- Protein: 20g
- Carbohydrates: 2g
- Fat: 14g

Ingredients:

- 1/2 cup almond flour
- 1/4 cup cocoa powder
- 1/4 teaspoon baking powder
- 1/4 cup unsalted butter, melted
- 1/2 cup granulated sweetener (such as erythritol)
- 2 eggs
- 1 teaspoon vanilla extract
- 1/4 cup chopped nuts (optional)

Instructions:

1. Preheat the oven to 350°F (175°C) and grease a baking dish.
2. In a bowl, whisk together almond flour, cocoa powder, and baking powder.
3. In another bowl, mix melted butter, sweetener, eggs, and vanilla extract until well combined.
4. Gradually add the dry ingredients to the wet ingredients, stirring until smooth.
5. Fold in chopped nuts, if using.
6. Pour the batter into the prepared baking dish and spread it evenly.
7. Bake for 20 minutes, or until a toothpick inserted into the center comes out clean.
8. Allow to cool before cutting into squares.

Protein Ice Cream

 Servings: 2 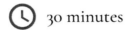 30 minutes

- *Calories: 180*
- *Protein: 20g*
- *Carbohydrates: 12g*
- *Fat: 5g*

Ingredients:

- 2 cups Greek yogurt
- 1 scoop protein powder (vanilla or chocolate flavor)
- 1 tablespoon honey or a low-carb sweetener
- 1 teaspoon vanilla extract
- Fresh fruit for topping

Instructions:

1. In a blender, combine Greek yogurt, protein powder, honey, and vanilla extract.
2. Blend until smooth and creamy.
3. Transfer the mixture to a shallow dish and freeze for at least 4 hours or until firm.
4. Scoop into bowls and top with fresh fruit before serving.

Berry Yogurt Parfait

 Servings: 2   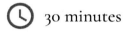 30 minutes

- Calories: 150
- Protein: 12g
- Carbohydrates: 20g
- Fat: 3g

Ingredients:

- 1 cup Greek yogurt
- 1/2 cup mixed berries (such as strawberries, blueberries, and raspberries)
- 1/4 cup granola (optional)
- 1 tablespoon honey or a low-carb sweetener
- Fresh mint leaves for garnish

Instructions:

1. In serving glasses, layer Greek yogurt, mixed berries, and granola if using.
2. Drizzle honey or sweetener over the top.
3. Refrigerate for at least 20 minutes to chill.
4. Garnish with fresh mint leaves before serving.

Chocolate Truffles

 Servings: 12   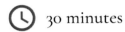 30 minutes

- *Calories: 120*
- *Protein: 2g*
- *Carbohydrates: 7g*
- *Fat: 10g*

Ingredients:

- 8 oz (225g) dark chocolate, chopped
- 1/2 cup heavy cream
- 1 tablespoon unsalted butter
- Cocoa powder or shredded coconut for coating

Instructions:

1. Place chopped dark chocolate in a heatproof bowl.
2. In a saucepan, heat heavy cream and butter until just simmering.
3. Pour the hot cream mixture over the chocolate and let it sit for 2 minutes.
4. Stir until smooth and well combined.
5. Cover and refrigerate for at least 2 hours, or until firm.
6. Once chilled, scoop out small portions and roll into balls.
7. Roll the truffles in cocoa powder or shredded coconut to coat.
8. Store in the refrigerator until ready to serve.

Coconut Macaroons

 Servings: 12    30 minutes

- Calories: 90
- Protein: 2g
- Carbohydrates: 4g
- Fat: 7g

Ingredients:

- 2 cups shredded coconut (unsweetened)
- 1/2 cup almond flour
- 1/4 cup granulated sweetener (such as erythritol)
- 2 egg whites
- 1 teaspoon vanilla extract
- Dark chocolate for drizzling (optional)

Instructions:

1. Preheat the oven to 325°F (160°C) and line a baking sheet with parchment paper.
2. In a bowl, mix together shredded coconut, almond flour, and sweetener.
3. In another bowl, beat the egg whites and vanilla extract until stiff peaks form.
4. Gently fold the egg whites into the coconut mixture until well combined.
5. Drop spoonfuls of the mixture onto the prepared baking sheet.
6. Bake for 20 minutes, or until golden brown.
7. Allow to cool completely before drizzling with dark chocolate, if desired.

Protein Chocolate Shake

 Servings: 1 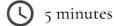 5 minutes

- *Calories: 150*
- *Protein: 20g*
- *Carbohydrates: 8g*
- *Fat: 4g*

Ingredients:

- 1 cup unsweetened almond milk
- 1 scoop chocolate protein powder
- 1 tablespoon cocoa powder
- 1/2 banana (optional)
- Ice cubes

Instructions:

1. In a blender, combine almond milk, protein powder, cocoa powder, banana if using, and ice cubes.
2. Blend until smooth and creamy.
3. Pour into a glass and serve immediately.

Fruit Salad with Protein

 Servings: 4   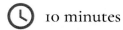 10 minutes

- Calories: 120
- Protein: 12g
- Carbohydrates: 18g
- Fat: 2g

Ingredients:

- 2 cups mixed fruit (such as berries, kiwi, and pineapple)
- 1/2 cup Greek yogurt
- 1 scoop vanilla protein powder
- Fresh mint leaves for garnish

Instructions:

1. In a bowl, combine mixed fruit.
2. In another bowl, mix Greek yogurt and vanilla protein powder until smooth.
3. Pour the yogurt mixture over the fruit and toss gently to coat.
4. Garnish with fresh mint leaves before serving.

Baked Apples with Nuts

 Servings: 4 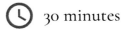 30 minutes

- *Calories: 150*
- *Protein: 2g*
- *Carbohydrates: 25g*
- *Fat: 6g*

Ingredients:

- 4 apples
- 1/4 cup chopped nuts (such as walnuts or pecans)
- 2 tablespoons honey or a low-carb sweetener
- 1 teaspoon cinnamon
- 1 tablespoon unsalted butter

Instructions:

1. Preheat the oven to 375°F (190°C) and grease a baking dish.
2. Core the apples and place them in the baking dish.
3. In a bowl, mix chopped nuts, honey, cinnamon, and butter.
4. Stuff each apple with the nut mixture.
5. Bake for 20 minutes, or until the apples are tender.
6. Serve warm.

Almond Cookies

 Servings: 12 25 minutes

- Calories: 90
- Protein: 2g
- Carbohydrates: 2g
- Fat: 8g

Ingredients:

- 1 cup almond flour
- 1/4 cup granulated sweetener (such as erythritol)
- 1/4 teaspoon baking soda
- 1/4 teaspoon salt
- 1/4 cup unsalted butter, melted
- 1 teaspoon vanilla extract
- 1 egg
- Sliced almonds for topping (optional)

Instructions:

1. Preheat the oven to 350°F (175°C) and line a baking sheet with parchment paper.
2. In a bowl, whisk together almond flour, sweetener, baking soda, and salt.
3. In another bowl, mix melted butter, vanilla extract, and egg until well combined.
4. Gradually add the dry ingredients to the wet ingredients, stirring until a dough forms.
5. Roll the dough into balls and place them on the prepared baking sheet.
6. Flatten each ball with the palm of your hand and press sliced almonds on top, if using.
7. Bake for 15 minutes, or until golden brown.
8. Allow to cool before serving.

Keto Tartlets

 Servings: 6 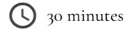 30 minutes

- *Calories: 120*
- *Protein: 3g*
- *Carbohydrates: 4g*
- *Fat: 10g*

Ingredients:

- 1 cup almond flour
- 2 tablespoons granulated sweetener (such as erythritol)
- 2 tablespoons unsalted butter, melted
- 1 egg
- 1/2 cup sugar-free raspberry jam
- Fresh raspberries for topping

Instructions:

1. Preheat the oven to 350°F (175°C) and grease a muffin tin.
2. In a bowl, mix together almond flour, sweetener, melted butter, and egg until a dough forms.
3. Divide the dough into 6 equal portions and press each portion into the bottom and up the sides of the muffin tin to form tart shells.
4. Bake for 10 minutes, then remove from the oven.
5. Spoon raspberry jam into each tart shell and return to the oven for another 10 minutes.
6. Allow to cool before removing from the muffin tin.
7. Top with fresh raspberries before serving.

Protein Muffins

 Servings: 6    🕐 30 minutes

- *Calories: 150*
- *Protein: 6g*
- *Carbohydrates: 4g*
- *Fat: 12g*

Ingredients:

- 1 cup almond flour
- 1 scoop protein powder (vanilla flavor)
- 1/4 cup granulated sweetener (such as erythritol)
- 1 teaspoon baking powder
- 1/4 teaspoon salt
- 2 eggs
- 1/4 cup unsweetened almond milk
- 1/4 cup melted coconut oil
- 1 teaspoon vanilla extract
- Fresh berries for topping

Instructions:

1. Preheat the oven to 350°F (175°C) and line a muffin tin with paper liners.
2. In a bowl, whisk together almond flour, protein powder, sweetener, baking powder, and salt.
3. In another bowl, beat eggs, almond milk, melted coconut oil, and vanilla extract until well combined.
4. Gradually add the dry ingredients to the wet ingredients, stirring until just combined.
5. Divide the batter evenly among the muffin cups.
6. Top each muffin with fresh berries.
7. Bake for 20 minutes, or until a toothpick inserted into the center comes out clean.
8. Allow to cool before serving.

Banana Protein Bread

 Servings: 8   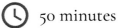 50 minutes

- *Calories: 180*
- *Protein: 8g*
- *Carbohydrates: 6g*
- *Fat: 14g*

Ingredients:

- 1 cup almond flour
- 1/4 cup coconut flour
- 1 scoop protein powder (vanilla flavor)
- 1 teaspoon baking powder
- 1/4 teaspoon baking soda
- 1/4 teaspoon salt
- 2 ripe bananas, mashed
- 2 eggs
- 1/4 cup melted coconut oil
- 1/4 cup Greek yogurt
- 1 teaspoon vanilla extract
- 1/4 cup chopped nuts (such as walnuts or pecans)

Instructions:

1. Preheat the oven to 350°F (175°C) and grease a loaf pan.
2. In a bowl, whisk together almond flour, coconut flour, protein powder, baking powder, baking soda, and salt.
3. In another bowl, mix mashed bananas, eggs, melted coconut oil, Greek yogurt, and vanilla extract until well combined.
4. Gradually add the dry ingredients to the wet ingredients, stirring until just combined.
5. Fold in chopped nuts.
6. Pour the batter into the prepared loaf pan.
7. Bake for 40 minutes, or until a toothpick inserted into the center comes out clean.
8. Allow to cool before slicing.

Berry Protein Pie

 Servings: 8   30 minutes

- *Calories: 150*
- *Protein: 5g*
- *Carbohydrates: 10g*
- *Fat: 10g*

Ingredients:
- 1 cup almond flour
- 1/4 cup coconut flour
- 1 scoop protein powder (vanilla flavor)
- 1/4 teaspoon salt
- 1/4 cup melted coconut oil
- 2 tablespoons honey or a low-carb sweetener
- 2 cups mixed berries (such as strawberries, blueberries, and raspberries)
- 1 tablespoon lemon juice
- Zest of 1 lemon
- 1 tablespoon arrowroot powder

Instructions:
1. Preheat the oven to 350°F (175°C).
2. In a bowl, mix together almond flour, coconut flour, protein powder, and salt.
3. Add melted coconut oil and honey, and mix until a dough forms.
4. Press the dough into a greased pie dish, covering the bottom and sides evenly.
5. In another bowl, toss mixed berries with lemon juice, lemon zest, and arrowroot powder.
6. Spoon the berry mixture into the pie crust.
7. Bake for 20 minutes, or until the crust is golden brown and the berries are bubbling.
8. Allow to cool before slicing.

Green Protein Smoothie

 Servings: 1   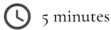 5 minutes

- *Calories: 250*
- *Protein: 25g*
- *Carbohydrates: 20g*
- *Fat: 8g*

Ingredients:

- 1 cup unsweetened almond milk
- 1 scoop vanilla protein powder
- 1/2 frozen banana
- 1 cup fresh spinach
- 1/2 tablespoon almond butter
- Ice cubes

Instructions:

1. In a blender, combine almond milk, protein powder, frozen banana, spinach, and almond butter.
2. Blend until smooth.
3. Add ice cubes and blend again until desired consistency is reached.
4. Pour into a glass and enjoy immediately.

Protein
Smoothie

with Berries

 Servings: 1    5 minutes

- *Calories: 220*
- *Protein: 25g*
- *Carbohydrates: 20g*
- *Fat: 7g*

Ingredients:

- 1 cup unsweetened almond milk
- 1 scoop vanilla protein powder
- 1/2 cup frozen mixed berries
- 1/2 banana
- 1 tablespoon chia seeds
- Ice cubes (optional)

Instructions:

1. Combine all ingredients in a blender.
2. Blend until smooth.
3. Pour into a glass and enjoy immediately.

Keto Latte

 Servings: 1   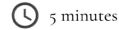 5 minutes

- *Calories: 150*
- *Protein: 1g*
- *Carbohydrates: 1g*
- *Fat: 15g*

Ingredients:

- 1 cup brewed coffee
- 1/4 cup unsweetened almond milk
- 1 tablespoon MCT oil or coconut oil
- 1 tablespoon heavy cream
- 1/2 teaspoon vanilla extract
- Stevia or other low-carb sweetener to taste

Instructions:

1. Brew a cup of coffee and pour it into a blender.
2. Add almond milk, MCT oil, heavy cream, vanilla extract, and sweetener to the blender.
3. Blend until frothy.
4. Pour into a mug and enjoy.

Ginger Lemon Tea

 Servings: 1   🕐 10 minutes

- *Calories: 5*
- *Protein: 0g*
- *Carbohydrates: 1g*
- *Fat: 0g*

Ingredients:

- 1 cup water
- 1 inch fresh ginger, sliced
- 1/2 lemon, juiced
- Stevia or other low-carb sweetener to taste

Instructions:

1. In a small saucepan, bring water to a boil.
2. Add sliced ginger to the boiling water and reduce the heat to low.
3. Simmer for 5 minutes.
4. Remove from heat and strain out the ginger slices.
5. Stir in lemon juice and sweetener to taste.
6. Pour into a mug and serve hot.

Chocolate Protein Shake

 Servings: 1 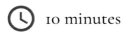 10 minutes

- *Calories: 200*
- *Protein: 25g*
- *Carbohydrates: 15g*
- *Fat: 5g*

Ingredients:

- 1 cup unsweetened almond milk
- 1 scoop chocolate protein powder
- 1 tablespoon unsweetened cocoa powder
- 1/2 frozen banana
- Ice cubes

Instructions:

1. In a blender, combine almond milk, protein powder, cocoa powder, frozen banana, and ice cubes.
2. Blend until smooth and creamy.
3. Pour into a glass and enjoy immediately.

Workout Guide for Maximizing Muscle Building

Beginner Workout:

This workout guide complements our book by offering customized exercise programs for three different fitness levels: beginner, intermediate, and advanced. Each level includes exercises that promote muscle growth and complement a high-protein diet, allowing readers to effectively achieve their fitness goals.

Warm-Up:

- Goal: To increase heart rate and blood flow to muscles, preparing them for exercise.
- Routine: Begin with 5 minutes of light cardio such as jogging in place, jumping jacks, or brisk walking. This helps to elevate body temperature and lubricate joints.

Strength Training:

1. **Squats:**
   - Muscles Targeted: Quadriceps, hamstrings, glutes, and core.
   - Description: Stand with feet hip-width apart, toes slightly turned out. Bend knees and hips to lower your body as if sitting back into a chair. Keep chest up and back straight. Lower until thighs are parallel to the ground. Push through heels to return to standing.
   - **Repetitions**: Start with 2 sets of 10-12 repetitions.

Push-Ups:

- Muscles Targeted: Chest, shoulders, triceps, and core.
- Description: Start in a plank position with hands slightly wider than shoulder-width apart. Lower body until chest nearly touches the floor, elbows pointing back at a 45-degree angle. Push back up to starting position.
- **Repetitions:** Perform 2 sets of 8-10 repetitions. Modify by kneeling if needed.

Lunges:

Muscles Targeted: Quadriceps, hamstrings, glutes, and core.
Description: Stand with feet hip-width apart. Step forward with one leg, lowering your hips until both knees are bent at a 90-degree angle. Front knee should not go past toes. Push back to starting position.
Repetitions: Perform 2 sets of 10 lunges on each leg.

Planks:

- Muscles Targeted: Core muscles (abdominals, obliques), shoulders, and back.
- Description: Start in a push-up position, but with forearms on the ground. Keep body in a straight line from head to heels, engaging core muscles. Hold for 20-30 seconds initially, increasing duration as strength improves.
- **Repetitions:** Aim for 2 sets of 20-30 seconds.

Dumbbell Rows:

Muscles Targeted: Upper back, lats, and biceps.
Description: Stand with feet hip-width apart, holding a dumbbell in each hand. Hinge at the hips, keeping back flat and chest up. Pull dumbbells towards hips, squeezing shoulder blades together. Lower back down with control.
Repetitions: Perform 2 sets of 10-12 repetitions.

Duration and Frequency:

- Duration: Each session should last 20-30 minutes, including warm-up and cool-down stretches.
- Frequency: Aim for 2-3 sessions per week, allowing at least one day of rest between sessions to promote muscle recovery and growth.

Note:

Beginners should focus on mastering proper form and gradually increasing intensity. Start with lighter weights or bodyweight exercises to avoid injury and build a strong foundation for future workouts. Regular consistency and proper technique are key to progressing safely and effectively in strength training.

Intermediate Workout:

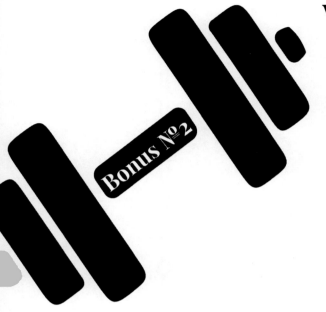

Warm-Up:

- Goal: Prepare muscles and joints for higher intensity exercises, increasing heart rate and blood flow.
- Routine: Perform 5-10 minutes of dynamic stretches such as leg swings, arm circles, high knees, and butt kicks. Follow with light cardio like jogging or jumping rope to further warm up the body.

Strength Training:

Deadlifts:

- Muscles Targeted: Hamstrings, glutes, lower back, and core.
- Description: Stand with feet hip-width apart, toes under the barbell. Hinge at hips and bend knees slightly to grasp the barbell with hands shoulder-width apart. Keep back straight, chest up, and shoulders back. Lift barbell by extending hips and knees, then lower back down with control.
- **Repetitions:** Perform 3 sets of 8-10 repetitions.

Bench Press:

- Muscles Targeted: Chest, shoulders, and triceps.
- Description: Lie on a flat bench with feet flat on the floor. Grip the barbell slightly wider than shoulder-width apart. Lower the bar to chest level, elbows at about 45 degrees. Push the bar back up until arms are fully extended.
- **Repetitions:** Perform 3 sets of 8-10 repetitions.

Pull-Ups:

- Muscles Targeted: Latissimus dorsi, biceps, and upper back.
- Description: Grip a pull-up bar with palms facing away from you, slightly wider than shoulder-width apart. Pull your body up until your chin clears the bar, keeping core engaged and elbows close to the body. Lower yourself back down with control.
- **Repetitions:** Perform 3 sets of as many repetitions as possible (aim for 6-10 repetitions).

Overhead Press:

- Muscles Targeted: Shoulders, triceps, and upper chest.
- Description: Stand with feet hip-width apart, holding a barbell or dumbbells at shoulder height with palms facing forward. Press the weight overhead until arms are fully extended. Lower back down with control.
- Repetitions: Perform 3 sets of 8-10 repetitions.

Kettlebell Swings:

- Muscles Targeted: Glutes, hamstrings, core, and shoulders.
- Description: Stand with feet shoulder-width apart, holding a kettlebell with both hands in front of hips. Hinge at hips, swinging kettlebell between legs, then thrust hips forward to swing kettlebell up to shoulder height. Allow kettlebell to swing back down between legs, controlling the movement.
- Repetitions: Perform 3 sets of 15-20 repetitions.

Duration and Frequency:

- Duration: Each session should last 30-45 minutes, including warm-up and cool-down stretches.
- Frequency: Aim for 3-4 sessions per week, with at least one day of rest between sessions to allow muscles to recover and grow stronger.

Note:

Intermediate workouts focus on increasing intensity and challenging muscles with compound exercises using moderate weights. Proper form and technique are crucial to prevent injury and maximize muscle engagement. Progressively increase weights as strength improves to continue stimulating muscle growth effectively.

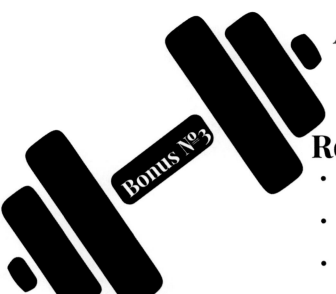

Bonus №3

Advanced Workout:

Goal: Optimize muscle growth and strength with advanced exercises.

Routine:

- Warm-Up: 10 minutes including dynamic stretches and cardio drills.
- Strength Training: High-intensity exercises with heavy weights, focusing on progressive overload.
- Duration: 45-60 minutes per session, 4-5 sessions per week.

Squat Variations (e.g., Front Squats, Back Squats):

- Description: Front squats involve holding a barbell in front of shoulders while performing squats. Back squats use a barbell across the back of shoulders.
- Muscles Targeted: Similar to basic squats but with increased load on quadriceps, hamstrings, glutes, and core.
- Benefits: Enhances lower body strength and power, improves overall athletic performance.

Barbell Rows:

- Description: Stand with feet hip-width apart, knees slightly bent, and bend forward at hips. Grip barbell with palms facing down, pull barbell toward torso, squeezing shoulder blades together.
- Muscles Targeted: Upper back (rhomboids, trapezius), biceps.
- Benefits: Builds upper back strength, promotes better posture, enhances pulling strength.

Military Press:

- Description: Stand with feet hip-width apart and hold the barbell at shoulder height with palms facing forward. Press the barbell overhead until arms are fully extended, then lower back down.
- Muscles Targeted: Shoulders (deltoids), triceps, core for stability.
- Benefits: Develops shoulder strength and stability, improves upper body pressing power.

Weighted Pull-Ups:

- Description: Attach weight around waist or hold dumbbell between feet during traditional pull-up motion (palms facing away). Pull body upward until chin is above bar, then lower back down.
- Muscles Targeted: Back (latissimus dorsi, teres major), biceps, core.
- Benefits: Increases pulling strength, promotes muscle hypertrophy in upper back and arms

Box Jumps:

- Description: Stand facing sturdy box or platform. Jump onto box with both feet, ensuring full hip and knee extension at top. Step or jump back down to starting position.
- Muscles Targeted: Lower body (quadriceps, hamstrings, calves), core for stabilization.
- Benefits: Enhances explosive power, improves lower body strength and coordination.

Weekly Workout Schedule

Monday - Upper Body Strength

- **Warm-Up:**

10 minute

- **Main Workout:**
  1. Barbell Bench Press: 4 sets x 8-10 reps
  2. Bent-Over Rows: 4 sets
  3. Dumbbell Shoulde
  4. Pull-Ups (or Assisted Pull-Ups): 3 sets x max reps

Cool Down: 5 minutes of static stretching for chest, back, and shoulders.

Tuesday - Lower Body Strength

- **Warm-Up:**

10 minutes of dynamic stretches and light cardio.

- **Main Workout:**
  1. Back Squats: 4 sets x 8-10 reps
  2. Romanian Deadlifts: 4 sets x 8-10 reps
  3. Lunges (weighted or bodyweight): 3 sets x 10-12 reps per leg
  4. Calf Raises: 3 sets x 15-20 reps

Cool Down: 5 minutes of static stretching for legs and hips.

Wednesday - Active Recovery

- Activity: Light cardio (walking, swimming, cycling) or yoga/stretching for 30-40 minutes to promote recovery.

Thursday - Push Day

- **Warm-Up:**

10 minutes of dynamic stretches and light cardio.

- **Main Workout:**
  1. Military Press (Barbell or Dumbbell): 4 sets x 8-10 reps
  2. Incline Bench Press: 4 sets x 8-10 reps
  3. Tricep Dips: 3 sets x 10-12 reps
  4. Lateral Raises: 3 sets x 12-15 reps

Cool Down: 5 minutes of static stretching for shoulders, chest, and triceps.

Friday - Pull Day

- **Warm-Up:**

10 minutes of dynamic stretches and light cardio.

- **Main Workout:**
  1. Deadlifts: 4 sets x 6-8 reps
  2. Pull-Ups (or Assisted Pull-Ups): 4 sets x max reps
  3. Seated Rows: 3 sets x 10-12 reps
  4. Bicep Curls (Barbell or Dumbbell): 3 sets x 12-15 reps

Cool Down: 5 minutes of static stretching for back and biceps.

Saturday - Lower Intensity Cardio and Core

- **Activity:** 30-40 minutes of moderate intensity cardio (jogging, cycling) or low-impact activities (swimming, brisk walking).
- **Core Workout:**
  1. Planks: 3 sets x 30-45 seconds
  2. Russian Twists: 3 sets x 20 reps per side
  3. Leg Raises: 3 sets x 12-15 reps
- **Cool Down:** 5 minutes of static stretching for core muscles.

Sunday - Rest Day

- **Rest and Recovery:** Allow time for muscles to repair and replenish. Focus on adequate hydration and nutrition to support recovery.

Adjust the weights and intensity of exercises based on your fitness level and progression. Ensure proper form and technique to prevent injuries and maximize workout effectiveness.

Disclaimer

The information in "Your Ultimate Low Carb High Protein Cookbook for Weight Loss and Muscle Building" is only for educational and informational purposes. The recipes and workout routines in this book are designed to support a healthy lifestyle, but they are not a substitute for professional medical advice, diagnosis, or treatment. Always seek the advice of your physician or other qualified health provider with any questions you may have regarding a medical condition or before starting any new diet or exe

The authors and publishers of this book are not responsible for any adverse effects or consequences resulting from the use of any recipes or workout routines suggested in this book. All readers are encouraged to use their own discretion and consult with a healthcare professional when necessary.

Copyright

First Edition: June 2024

ABIGAIL ATKINSON

Made in the USA
Las Vegas, NV
13 December 2024

14181821R00057